THE MAGICAL

TURKEY

AND

DAD

Sukhdev Kaur Dosanjh

One chilly morning, Dad said, 'Let's make a turkey dinner like no other!' But this wasn't just any turkey...

With a *poof*, the turkey was wearing a tiny hat and glasses! 'Hello!' it said cheerfully. Dad and I looked at each other. 'Did that turkey just talk?' I whispered.

'Follow me!' said the magical turkey.

And he led us to a shimmering door that had appeared in the wall.

We stepped through the door and found ourselves in a forest made of mashed potatoes!

We jumped from one fluffy mashed potato cloud to the next, laughing as we bounced.

'These are cranberry bushes!' the turkey said, picking a bunch for us to taste.

The cranberries sparkled, tasting sweeter and juicier than anything we'd ever had!

Then, we came to a river of gravy! The turkey handed Dad a tiny boat and said, 'Hop in!'

We floated along, dipping our hands in the warm, tasty gravy as we sailed.

Suddenly, we saw a castle in the distance, made entirely of stuffing!'Welcome to the Stuffing Castle!' announced the turkey, bowing grandly.

The hall was filled with every thanksgiving food you could imagine!

There were sparkling chandeliers of popcorn and walls made of golden corn.

We met a dancing cranberry, a giggling pie, and a choir of sweet potatoes singing in harmony!

We all danced together, spinning and laughing with our new food friends.

In the throne room, a giant pie greeted us.
'I am the King of the Feast!' he
proclaimed.

The King Pie cut a slice for each of us, and it was the most delicious pie we'd ever tasted!

'Uh-oh,' said the turkey. 'It's almost time for you to go back home!'

The turkey opened another door, glowing like the first one, and led us through it. We waved goodbye to our magical friends, promising to never forget this adventure.

We were back in the kitchen, with our turkey sitting on the table like nothing had happened.

'Was it all a dream?' Dad asked, but we both knew it was real. I reached into my pocket and pulled out a small, sparkly feather. Proof of our adventure! We sat down together, ready for a meal, feeling grateful for our magical friend.

And if you looked closely, you might have seen the turkey give a little wink.

We laughed and told the story again, remembering every magical moment.

]

That night, I put the feather on my bedside table, wondering if we'd ever go back..

As I drifted off to sleep, I dreamed of the next adventure waiting for us.

The end...

or maybe just the beginning!

www.googni.com

Made in United States
Orlando, FL
22 November 2024

54298193R00015